"The Willis brothers have inspirationally opened my mind and eyes to horizons I had once never imagined. Milton and Michael have perpetuated the spirit of my life through their thoughts and words. So I guess you could say, I owe them my life. They have changed it for the best."
— Jason Kozlik, Web technician, Solana Beach, CA

"In my thirty years of teaching, the Willis brothers' essays are the best way I have found to teach students core values and positive life lessons. Inspirational, educational, and informative messages delivered through popular culture and sports! Genius!"
— Cheryl Reynolds, teacher, Rutland, VT

"I especially like their belief system and incorporating surfing into daily life."
— David Beadle, work/life coordinator, Qualcomm

"The stories and writings of the Willis brothers significantly benefit my personal and professional life. They provide engaging lessons that I can apply at home with my kids as well as in the workplace."
— Martin Rips, San Diego, CA

"Thanks to the Willis brothers and their philosophy... I now have a totally new perspective on life."
— Amy Pickell, grant writer, Rancho Bernardo, CA

"The Willis brothers are dedicated people with a great deal of experience teaching surfing and the virtues of being in harmony with nature."
— Eric Roudi, CEO, OpenWorks, Scottsdale, AZ

"The Willis brothers exemplify the spirit of surfing."
— Surfing Magazine

"Every time I think of the Willis bro   *h the spirit of loving life. They have succe*   *e not only how to surf waves in the ocean,*   *d surf the many waves of life."*

....ne.com

"The Willis brothers truly capture how the lessons learned in the ocean can apply to life."
— Shawn Styles, KFMB Television

Blue Mountain Arts®

Bestselling Titles

By Susan Polis Schutz:
To My Daughter, with Love, on the Important Things in Life
To My Son with Love

By Douglas Pagels:
30 Beautiful Things That Are True About You
42 Gifts I'd Like to Give to You
100 Things to Always Remember... and One Thing to Never Forget
May You Always Have an Angel by Your Side
To the One Person I Consider to Be My Soul Mate

Is It Time to Make a Change?
by Deanna Beisser

I Prayed for You Today
To the Love of My Life
by Donna Fargo

Anthologies:
Always Believe in Yourself and Your Dreams
For You, My Daughter
Friends for Life
Hang In There
I Love You, Mom
I'm Glad You Are My Sister
The Joys and Challenges of Motherhood
The Language of Recovery
Marriage Is a Promise of Love
Teaching and Learning Are Lifelong Journeys
There Is Greatness Within You, My Son
Think Positive Thoughts Every Day
Thoughts to Share with a Wonderful Teenager
True Wealth
With God by Your Side ...You Never Have to Be Alone
You're Just like a Sister to Me

Discover the
Greatness
in
You

Words of
Wisdom and Empowerment
to Help You Become the Person
You Are Meant to Be

Milton Willis and Michael Willis

Blue Mountain Press ™

Boulder, Colorado

Library of Congress Catalog Card Number: 2005037427
ISBN: 1-59842-069-0

Certain trademarks are used under license.
BLUE MOUNTAIN PRESS is registered in U.S. Patent and Trademark Office.

Printed in the United States of America.
First Printing: 2006

 This book is printed on recycled paper.

This book is printed on fine quality, laid embossed, 80 lb. paper. This paper has been specially produced to be acid free (neutral pH) and contains no groundwood or unbleached pulp. It conforms with all the requirements of the American National Standards Institute, Inc., so as to ensure that this book will last and be enjoyed by future generations.

Library of Congress Cataloging-in-Publication Data

Willis, Milton, 1956-
Discover the greatness in you : words of wisdom and empowerment
to help you become the person you are meant to be / Milton Willis and
Michael Willis.
      p. cm.
      ISBN 1-59842-069-0 (trade pbk. : alk. paper)
  1. Self-actualization (Psychology) 2. Surfing—Miscellanea.
  I. Willis, Michael, 1956 -   . II. Title.
BF637.S4W55 2006
158.1— dc22

                                                2005037427

Blue Mountain Arts, Inc.
P.O. Box 4549, Boulder, Colorado 80306

Introduction

The human mind is an endless ocean where every thought is a wave and everyone is a surfer. Some people are overwhelmed by the challenge of the waves and never find the courage, faith, or knowledge to leave the safety and security of the shore. Others are already in the surf but desire to rise to higher levels. The purpose of this book is to help those who want to get off the beach and into the waves of life. It is also to show those already in the surf how to draw strength from within and get the most out of every wave.

Imagine, your dream wave is out there now. It is coming this way. It's right in front of you — calling your name, beckoning you to paddle out and catch it. It may be easy to ride or it may be difficult. Either way, once you take a chance and discover the surfer inside you, you will be prepared to catch all kinds of waves and look at life in a new and refreshing way.

Some people ride high on the swells of triumph, well-being, and success. For these surfers, it is as if they can look into the future and see the invisible. Even the most awe-inspiring, challenging, and perilous waves appear effortless. Others face major challenges, wipeouts, and adversity, but no matter how insurmountable obstacles seem, nothing stops them. They rely on experience, knowledge, and simple actions to get them through the longest rides. They have learned to face and overcome their biggest challenges and fears with courage, faith, and self-control even in extremely out-of-control situations. You can, too.

Whatever kind of wave you are surfing, you can realize your dreams by being in the right place at the right time doing the right thing — starting with the right thought. The most powerful waves are found in the ocean of the mind. This book is a surfing lesson for successfully navigating the waves of life.

So why not take a chance? Open this book to any page and see how positively it speaks to you. Think about how the thoughts and ideas presented here can apply to many aspects of your life. *Discover the Greatness in You* will equip you with relevant insights as well as a fresh, new perspective on life, similar to the feeling of going surfing. Every time you read this book, you are paddling back out. You're surfing! Life is surfing. Make it happen. Believe in yourself, and soon you will be surfing waves in the ocean where dreams come true.

— *Milton Willis*
Michael Willis

Endless **waves** of love,

happiness, and harmony

await all who dare to go

for their **dreams**.

It requires a heart filled

with **courage**

and a soul overflowing

with **hope**.

A life well lived influences
and inspires others
to **reach out**
and live their dreams.

If one person believes in
something **wholeheartedly**,
that person can
bring about **change**.

Dare to live your dreams

On the wave of life, the ride begins when we dare to live our dreams. So dream big. Dream of peace and brotherhood and a better tomorrow for all starting today. Dream for families to become stronger; dream of justice, equality, and happiness for all. Above all have hope. The time to dream is now; the time to live is now; the time to make a positive difference is now.

In order to live a dream, you must first reach for it with your full commitment, heart, and soul. It takes courage to go after lofty aspirations, especially if they seem impossible. If you desire to do or experience something for the first time, let nothing impede your forward progress. To realize honorable, pure, and noble dreams, you first have to go for them.

Breakthroughs occur
by taking chances.
Even when **things** seem
not to work out,
they do work out
if you remain **positive**.

Take a chance on life

Keep in mind that in every victory, every pursuit, you first have to take a chance. You will experience something you cannot get anywhere else or purchase with money: a chance to expand your mind, reality, and self-awareness... a chance to experience personal growth and live life to the fullest.

When it comes to personal challenge, the bigger the chance, the greater the reward. The secret to taking chances is to stack the odds in your favor as best you can. If you are prepared to handle and learn when things don't go your way, you will benefit regardless of the outcome.

Take a chance on life. It's through taking chances that significant personal growth, knowledge, and advancement take place. Believe in and trust yourself. Life is a chance. Take a chance.

In the quest for your dreams, begin with a clear vision...

The chances of successfully shaping a dream life are substantially higher when you have a clear vision and define your goals and aspirations ahead of time. The best way to implement your vision is to draw up workable plans that can be adjusted or revised as the goal takes form.

Never rely on luck. Once goals are established and plans for attaining desired results are in place, the shaping of your dream life starts. This is where the fun begins by seeing the shape of your vision or goals materializing right in front of you.

Put magic in your life
by having the foresight
to **visualize** what you want,
the insight to put together
a **plan** for success,
and the faith
to **follow it through**.

Inevitably, the goals and desires
that **shape** your **dreams**
will be realized.

Wholehearted, unwavering commitment is how people become great

Experienced surfers have a term for those who appear to be trying to catch waves but never do. They're called "rubber arms." Rubber arms are surfers who turn to catch a wave, making all the paddling movements, but never really go anywhere. Surfers who are rubber arms don't really want to drop in; the situation is much too intense. Many times, they experience some of the worst wipeouts. This is the price paid for not being fully committed and putting out a halfhearted effort.

When we commit ourselves to school, relationships, work, or anything else, we set the stage for unequivocal success. Without true commitment, we are just like a surfer who rubber arms. We go through the motions never fooling anyone, not even ourselves.

Halfhearted effort in anything will only result in disaster. When we commit to our goals, aspirations, hopes, and dreams, doubt and fear totally disappear, and we finish what we start. The characteristics of being one hundred percent committed are fortitude, truth, and inner strength.

Those who maintain and hold fast to their commitments, finishing what they start even in the darkest moments, will be the ones rewarded with unlimited success that borders on miraculous.

It's through **desire**
and **knowledge**,
combined with **action**,
that all things are
possible.

The most important quality to possess is desire.

Knowledge is the nutrition the mind needs to grow. Anyone can succeed at anything, provided they know what they are doing.

Simple actions based on accurate knowledge and compassion have the power to transform families, communities, and nations.

The vision is clear: With real knowledge and desire come real understanding and real success.

Everyone has to begin sometime

Standing on the shoreline of life, we all gaze longingly into the deep blue ocean of our dreams. We can choose to head out faithfully into a destiny yet to be realized or be held back by fears and never leave the shore.

No one starts out a master of his or her craft. In fact, each step of the way master crafters begin anew from where they left off. They realize they are perfect being imperfect; there is perfection in imperfection. By beginning again, each time the experience is always fresh, exciting, and forever new.

Never be intimidated by others. Everyone had to begin at one time or another.

Gain inner confidence you never knew you had through understanding, trust, and intuition, enabling you to stack the odds in your favor.

Above all, learn to trust yourself and your intuition. Listen closely to the voice inside you. If you really don't feel confident for any reason, don't be coerced into going into any situation you're not comfortable with. Before you commit to anything, make sure it feels right. There will always be another day. Trust yourself.

It takes willpower to win

Everyone can increase his or her chances of winning in life by developing the will to win and working for victory.

For some people, competition is everything and their will to win is intense. They live and breathe to win contests. Those at the top fully put their will into mind, body, and soul in hot pursuit of winning. Driven by sheer will, they work intensely and exclusively with only one purpose: success. They will not tire in this pursuit nor become discouraged.

Willpower produces the strength to endure. It is one of the most powerful forces known to mankind and the real beginning of all success.

Never let defeat stand in the way of your progress or dampen your will to win. In fact, let temporary defeat strengthen your will and resolve to win.

Winning is not an accident; winning is a result—the result of willpower and the hard work it takes to win. Winning is a full-time pursuit. Winners increase their chances of winning by having the will to win and doing the work it takes to win.

The "w" in win stands for work. It takes hard work to be a winner. There are no shortcuts to victory. A strong and positive will is crucial to winning.

Willpower turns temporary defeats into long-lasting advantages.

Motivation... a fire inside fueled by desire

When you are strongly motivated by and do what you honestly love, you will be compelled and driven by an unseen set of forces resulting in a life overflowing with meaning and substance.

When you are compelled toward a positive goal, neither fear nor finances nor any other would-be obstacles get in the way. Everything becomes possible.

Compare two different artists: One artist paints because she is inspired and compelled; the other waits for a commission fee to get started and doesn't pick up a brush purely for the love of painting. A great body of work comes from many artists whose only payment was they got to work.

Compelled individuals do things because they want to and feel they have to. When someone is compelled to achieve positive goals, they press forward because they have to. It's what they do. Reward is not found in fortune and fame but rather in realizing a dream.

Those who are compelled allow nothing to stop them from fulfilling their personal aspirations and life dreams. These are the ones who experience life at its fullest.

A great teacher can make a world of difference

Great teachers care, have extreme patience with others, extensive knowledge of their subject, and a deep understanding of how to disseminate information.

Patience is essential in teaching. A kind and patient teacher can help make learning thoroughly more pleasant and enjoyable while substantially increasing the effectiveness of the lesson. If a teacher is patient with a student, then that student will become patient, taking the time to do things correctly with confidence. If a teacher is short on patience, students quickly become nervous and make mistakes in haste, starting with being impatient.

When someone expertly and gently teaches from the heart what he or she knows in the head, knowledge transference will happen. By being patient and taking time to teach and to learn, positive, long-lasting results will be achieved much quicker. Whoever is lucky enough to learn from a patient teacher walks away a better and improved person.

In a way, everyone is a student as well as a teacher at one time or another — usually simultaneously. The student teaches the teacher how to teach better and helps the sincere teacher understand his or her subject better.

The teacher who teaches for real compensation — the joy of helping others succeed — will be caring, patient, knowledgeable, and understanding. Teachers are successful when they care, when they help change and impact other lives positively, regardless of the subject at hand. Specific lessons are sometimes less important than the lessons learned by the way one is taught.

A great teacher is of much greater value than the knowledge that teacher possesses, which is invaluable.

The ocean as teacher

Imagine a teacher who is as old as Earth and whose lessons have been proven time after time, a teacher with relentless patience.

With greater strength and power than all the armies of the world, the ocean has a profound effect on every form of life that has ever existed and teaches all who listen. The ocean is one of mankind's best friends.

As with any great and powerful teacher, the ocean demands respect: respect for nature, our bodies, and life itself. Every lesson learned in the ocean can and should be practiced ashore and integrated into our daily lives. In this case, the respect we earnestly practice and feel extended to our families, teachers, country, and ourselves is the foundation of healthy minds. This high regard and special consideration for the ocean helps us to keep things in the proper perspective.

Rhythm, timing, and flow are some of the building blocks the ocean uses to teach and unveil the secrets of the universe and success. The vast, powerful ocean is truly one of our greatest teachers, offering fun, entertainment, education, and physical and mental challenges. The ocean continues to offer the gift of life on this planet as we know it.

Waves rise, roll, and return to whence they originated, a never-ending cycle of life not unlike our very own. A person who is trained to look can see what causes the waves, where they came from, and where they are going. If you want to learn about anything — poetry, martial arts, prosperity, friendship, love, or about life itself — learn from the waves.

Don't let fear hold you back

Fear denies some people the pleasure of reaching for their dreams. People in a fearful state tend to attract what it is they feel they are not prepared to handle. By tensing up and panicking, they often cause their own misfortunes. Valuable energy that could be focused toward a solution actually helps to create a nightmare.

An example is the surfer who upon seeing a huge wave coming at him freezes up instead of just paddling out to get past it. He has already projected his reality by imagining future events and how he sees them playing out. By staying in the present moment, this surfer could have easily realized that there was plenty of time to paddle over or around the oncoming waves of fate. His worst nightmare happens when the wave breaks right on his head, and now the real situation begins to get worse. From imagination, what was most feared became reality.

The **fear** of failure
that keeps some people
from going after their dreams
gives others
the **passion**
they will have for a lifetime.

Never give up hope

Wilma Rudolph was born prematurely and spent the majority of her childhood in bed. She suffered serious bouts of double pneumonia, whooping cough, measles, mumps, scarlet fever, chicken pox, and polio — a crippling disease that had no cure at the time. Her left leg was so badly affected she had to wear a brace. Some people said she would never be able to walk. No one will ever know how much Rudolph struggled to finally gain health, but the whole world now knows how strong she became. Wilma Rudolph was the first American woman to win three gold medals in track and field in a single Olympics, breaking records along the way. She helped pave the way for future female athletes to be undeniably recognized for athletic prowess, skill, and ability.

One accepts fate while at the same time attempting to influence the outcome with positive thought and action that begins with hope.

Accept your fate with courage, get through it with open eyes, and steadfastly hope for a positive outcome and a brighter tomorrow.

Slow down your mind and your actions

Do you ever feel rushed? Are you constantly chasing success? You're not alone. Cars, boats, jets, and even Internet communication are moving us faster and faster. Many adults and children are experiencing anxiety, stress, and other ailments that are time related.

When facing an uncomfortable or fearful situation, it's best to slow down and deal with the exact moment at hand rather than trying to rush. The faster you try to get through it, the longer it will appear to last. Slowing down and getting through each moment as it comes will allow you to rationally deal and get through each single moment, accelerating your chances for survival. Rather than focusing on the future or the past, focus on what you have to do to survive right now. Take it moment by moment, and before you know it things will be okay. Even if it seems to take an eternity, all things shall pass.

Try an experiment in your life: Slow down your mind and your actions. While driving on the freeway, slow down one or two miles per hour. You will get there faster. While saying good night or good morning to your loved ones, take just a little longer. You will find your relationships improve. When you give a hug, make it last a little longer. When working, take a little extra time. Your satisfaction and production will skyrocket. You will see immediate results and improvement in the quality of your life.

Be in the moment...

Through waiting and watching, you learn to identify opportunities that others perhaps didn't. You are able to seize the moment, catch it, and own it.

Learn to be patient, be aware, take action, and accomplish the seemingly impossible.

Be in the moment: Transcend time. Don't think ahead or behind. Don't rush or try to hurry the moment. It is during times of personal challenge that survival skills and the ability to adapt are often at their highest, resulting in a much greater self-awareness and personal growth.

...and stay focused

For success in achieving personal goals, embrace challenge, keep your mind held steadfast on desired results, and, most important, never give up.

The human mind can only think one thought at a time. When facing a mammoth challenge, you cannot afford even a micro-thought of doubt. If one thought of doubt or fear enters the mind, then it is all over. Instead of embracing the challenge, you will find yourself running away from it.

Definitely one of the best lessons learned is that by keeping the mind focused and positive, anything and everything is possible. Whatever your desire — to be a scholar, a millionaire, a great athlete, a fantastic parent, or anything else — approach it by embracing the challenge with unwavering focus on the results that you want, and never give up.

Develop awareness...

A good rule of thumb is to always expect the unexpected. The best way to handle the unexpected is to keep your eyes wide open, stay alert, and watch where you are going.

By using pragmatic judgment and super awareness, seemingly impossible situations become possible.

Each challenge we face offers an opportunity for us to experience and develop complete and full awareness.

Life flows as effortlessly as a wave when we are in sync with what's going on around us.

...and never underestimate the value of hard work

Count your blessings and embrace sacrifice with hard work, and you will experience the miracles firsthand of a life worth living. Practice humility and respect others, yourself, and the environment, and you will expand your personal boundaries beyond imagination. Like all great accomplishments, everything begins with struggle, sacrifice, and humility, and the rewards for those who persevere are priceless.

To become great at anything requires more than superior talent. It requires hours upon hours, weeks, and years of endless practice and dedication. Three key ingredients to achieving greatness are struggle, sacrifice, and humility.

Ride the waves of change

Plans and hopes sometimes don't turn out as we expect. Dashed upon the shore like a breaking wave, life can change instantly.

Use the disturbances and friction in your life to ride waves of change, waves of freedom, waves of expression. It will make all the difference for a smooth ride.

Embrace challenge and struggle with unshakable resolve to succeed, and you will develop inner and outer strength that can be acquired nowhere else.

Stay calm... The moment you start to go against the flow is the moment when confidence and hope fly out the window.

Every step of the way, every moment, there is challenge inside of chance. No longer lingering over our shoulders, chance and destiny meet face to face. Sometimes more change happens in a split second than in ten thousand years.

In essence, life is a flowing wave. How you surf it will determine your destiny. Those who persevere in the face of adversity by remaining in control will gain confidence, strength, and courage, increasing all chances of success.

The difficult times will make you stronger

One's true character shines out in the darkest moments. This is when we come face to face with who we thought we were and who we really are. Core and personal life values surface when things are down and we are confronted with our own possible tragedy. A wise old surfer once said, "It's not the high moments that will define your life, but rather the ones filled with trials and the way you deal with them. How you handle the difficult times shows the real essence and measure of your true character. You will know more about yourself in times of trouble than at any other time."

Being faced with adversity provides a prime opportunity for real growth, deeper self-understanding, and long-lasting personal advancement.

Difficult times shape our attitudes and the way we view life, allowing us to deal or cope better in all moments. They build character and help us to become better, stronger, and more complete. After a difficult time, you learn to appreciate when things are going well. German philosopher Friedrich Nietzsche noted, "What doesn't destroy me makes me stronger." By going through difficult times, we learn to go beyond our present ability, extending our comfort zone, and becoming stronger along the way: physically, mentally, and spiritually.

Those who go through and survive turbulent times learn the lessons of humility, appreciation, and respect, gaining faith, wisdom, and real confidence as a result.

Accept defeat and move on

Some of us will experience waves of glory and success, while others will know the impact of disaster. Everyone has their day when they can do no wrong, and everyone suffers defeat sometimes. But life wouldn't be exciting if there were no challenges, and there wouldn't be any reason to focus or anything to learn. A perfect world in which defeat did not exist would not be perfect at all.

Defeat is nature's way of keeping us alert and waking us up. When it occurs, it is time to look around to see what is happening. Every failure or defeat offers us an opportunity for growth and teaches us life lessons firsthand, resulting in greater understanding and improved situations.

Everyone shines brightly when things go right. It's when things go wrong that we learn and gain true courage and strength.

Through enduring faith, a positive attitude, and incredible determination, it is possible to move from within the dark shadows of a breaking wave into the sunlight of success.

No matter how intense the defeat is, believe in yourself. Believe you will get through it. Failures are life's way of building character, strength, and insight.

Don't let life's waves catch you by surprise

Three surfers were having a great time waiting for some waves together. When it came to positioning themselves, the first and second surfers chose to line up off the third and most experienced surfer. The third surfer had carefully selected his spot based on "invisible" ocean maps — the leftover sea foam from previous breaking waves sometimes referred to as "bubble lines." The bubbles were there for everyone to see, but the others didn't know their value and never took notice.

The first surfer expertly judged the swells as they rolled by. He was looking for the right wave to catch that would give him a nice, long ride. The second surfer was a little more experienced. Using the rhythmic rise and fall of the waves to his advantage, he floated up with the swell to see the coming waves. Because of the rapid rise and fall of the waves, he had to make swift calculations and did not take the time to look farther out.

The third and most experienced surfer sat slightly farther out than the others. He also used the rise and fall of the swells to his advantage. Watching the waves as they went by, he was able to see how they were breaking and the direction they were going. When the swell floated him up, he would look not just at the following waves but also far out to the horizon, seeing waves well before they came.

A large series of oncoming waves started to come in. The first surfer, slightly out of position, started paddling as hard as he could for the lead wave. Alas, he missed it and was caught by the following waves, which pounded, churned, and spun him like a washing machine all the way to shore. He was lucky to survive, and his surfboard was broken in three places. He never saw the waves coming.

The second surfer made it over the first wave to see that the following waves were much larger and farther out than he had anticipated. Unfortunately he was out of position to catch the next wave and was consumed in an explosion of white water that violently tossed and turned him halfway to shore before he could come up for air. His surfboard ended up cracked in half. He saw the waves coming but not in time.

Sitting in perfect position, the third surfer caught the wave of the day and expertly surfed it all the way in, where he stepped off onto shore without even getting his hair wet. Putting his pristine surfboard under his arm, he made his way up the beach to join the others who were now all safely on shore. The third surfer was prepared ahead of time because he had the foresight to be aware and remain vigilant. He saw the waves coming well ahead of time, thus effectively seeing the future.

With a little **practice**,
using foresight and intuition
becomes second nature.
The trick to being
in the right time and place
is to remain **aware**,
look beyond,
and **be ready** for
whatever happens.

Try to think ahead

Champion athletes don't wait until the moment to deliver, they anticipate and already know what they will do when the moment arrives.

Take the sport of baseball. A good fielder knows ahead of time where the play will be if the ball is hit to him. He has already gone over every possible scenario. If a player waits until the ball is hit to him to decide what to do, he will have missed the moment. Learn to expand the present moment forward and outward to enable accurate insight into the future.

The best way to be prepared for the waves life sends your way is to have foresight, be aware, and remain vigilant. If you don't see waves coming ahead of time, you just might get caught by them. If you do see waves in advance, you will be prepared to catch the ride of your life!

Unite with others in a common goal

Humans can learn by observing how well California's brown pelicans work together and take turns leading. These pelicans use the updraft of incoming waves to surf their way up and down the coast. Smoothly soaring across open-faced waves, they form a line drafting off each other. Each individual pelican takes a turn in the front, breaking the wind for those following. They sail along until a wave begins to collapse. Then the lead pelican, followed by the others, will abruptly rise up and over the wave, descending to the next open-faced wave, and continue gliding on without ever missing a beat. Without saying a word, somehow the rear pelican knows instinctively when to rise up and take the lead.

Power is increased when families, corporations, and even countries work together... We are all related to every person alive today. Every living creature for that matter is part of one big, extended family.

It's said when one person works hand in hand with another, they are eleven times stronger.

When people unite for a common goal, dreams become reality... When people work together in harmony, fantastic things happen.

Through **teamwork**,
people have been able
to **accomplish**
personal miracles,
exceed limitations,
and extend mankind's
boundaries.

Whether your goals are to ride huge waves beyond imagination, to be the happiest person in the world, or other desires of the heart, possibilities of success increase with the support of a united team. To achieve anything, large or small, it helps to surround yourself with people who share common goals and work together in the spirit of unity. When two or more individuals get together harmoniously dedicated to the same cause, their strengths and powers are exponentially increased. The sum will be greater than its parts. Together we stand; divided we fall.

A team united with a common goal can turn a dream into reality.

It's when people get together that breakthroughs occur.

Hone your communication skills

To be a good communicator, it helps to practice communicating. If we only associate with people we know or only talk to people with our own interests and likes, everyone loses out. If you are older, you may want to have a conversation with someone younger. You may discover something you didn't know that could cause a positive change in your life. If music is your interest, talk with someone about sports, or vice versa. There is always something in common, even in the diverse.

If something is bothering you about a partner, friend, or family situation, don't hold it in. At work, develop relationships with those in positions above and below you. Receive as well as give information. Show your feelings and emotions for the benefit of all. The time to hone communication skills is now.

Clear, honest communication is essential for ourselves and others to maintain healthy, thriving relationships. The basis of all good communication is truth. If we are honest with ourselves, we will be honest with others.

Words and hand gestures are not our only forms of communication. Actions speak volumes, as well as facial expressions. Where there is open communication, you'll find harmony, prosperity, and peace. Where communication is lacking, there is usually disaster.

The better your communication skills, the greater chance you have of achieving your hopes, aspirations, and dreams for a better future.

Exceed expectations

Expert big-wave surfer Laird Hamilton is well-known and recognized for combining high-powered jet skis, giant waves, and surfing. He has paddled the English Channel as well as completed many long-distance paddles all over the world. An all-time great waterman, one of the many aspects that separates Hamilton from others is his ability to do things others haven't even dreamed of.

Gene "Tarzan" Smith is equally or even more amazing. He is best known as the first and only man to paddle from Oahu to Kauai on a thirteen-foot primitive wooden paddleboard, a historic feat of endurance, faith, and courage. It must have taken a lot of courage and no shortage of guts.

The genius of Gene "Tarzan" Smith and Laird Hamilton is that they didn't believe in simply following the standard, but instead chose to define, set, and exceed standards for past, present, and future generations.

If we each define and set
our own standards,
aiming higher and farther,
we will become conquerors,
expanding our inner and outer strengths
and **exceeding**
what we ever thought possible.

Genius lies in breaking new ground
or going where others have never gone.

Mankind is organic
and needs to stay
in touch
with **nature**
to be balanced
and **healthy**.
Being in nature
invigorates and
makes people feel alive.

Find a natural balance

Everywhere you look in nature, natural balance occurs: from the swirling planets to our individual lives. Natural balance keeps everything working in wondrous and perfect harmony.

One way to illustrate natural balance is to look at the wheel of a bicycle. If all the spokes are the same length and spread out just right, the wheel will roll smoothly. If even just one spoke is too short or long, the wheel cannot roll properly. Life is like this, too. For personal success, we need balance. The spokes of the wheel can represent activities and areas of our personal lives. If you give too much attention to work or pleasure, life will become unbalanced.

With balance come harmony, peace, and happiness.

The keys to achieving greatness

Struggle begets mental and physical strength... If you never give in to life's struggles, you will develop the muscle and mental fortitude to rise above challenges. The longer you endure, the deeper the reserves of strength there will be to rely on. Every great accomplishment that has ever occurred is the result of someone overcoming some type of struggle. In fact, for any activity or human endeavor to be considered great, it must involve some degree of struggle.

Sacrifice begets purity... It's through sacrifice that things and situations accrue their value. If you give up a lot to acquire something, it's going to mean a whole lot more than if it's given to you. When you sacrifice, work hard, and achieve something great, no one can take that satisfaction away from you. You've earned it. When someone actually earns an accomplishment, people are not jealous or envious; instead they are awe-inspired and moved. There is no such thing as a great accomplishment without sacrifice.

Humility begets respect... To be great, you have to experience and learn respect; this begins with being humble. Humility and respect come from feeling as if you are a part of something greater than yourself. Demonstrating respect shows you care, and when someone truly cares, fantastic things happen.

Struggle, sacrifice, and humility are the building blocks for all greatness... People experience struggle every single day. Those who struggle the hardest and yet persevere go on to do great things. Those who sacrifice understand the value of commitment and hard work and are willing to pay the price for real success that lasts. Society respects and loves those who remain humble even in victory. Those who have struggled and sacrificed don't have to have an attitude or brag. The results of their actions say it all.

A positive attitude is everything

Fate's manifestation is set in motion by what a person thinks, how a person feels, and the way a person deals with a situation.

All successful achievement has come from a single thought: I think I can. In life we help create our own triumphs and defeats depending on how and what we think.

What we think and believe will have a profound effect on all of us individually and collectively.

The mind is a very powerful thing, and by listening to our thoughts, we are able to tap into the unlimited power it has to offer.

Why use **valuable** life energy
entertaining thoughts of worry or doubt?
Thoughts of this kind will never help you
and can bring about havoc.
We are **keepers** of our own minds.
While we can't control what happens
around us, we can control our thoughts.
Victory in everything
first takes place in the mind.

Approach every aspect of your life with love

When we earnestly do the things we truly love, we are compelled, filled with endless enthusiasm and boundless strength. Hours fly by like seconds and life acquires real meaning.

The best athletes, businesspeople, artists, scientists, and others are usually self-motivated. They are inspired to do what they love. Their work is their life. You can hear it in Bach's music, see it in Picasso's paintings, or feel it when you see a surfer performing with full heart and soul.

Every action we take, every thought we think, and every feeling we feel is motivated by something. Motivation that comes from within and is generated from love is the most powerful. Performance inspired and motivated by love is always superior.

If you fully and honestly want something, put your heart into it. Sometimes victory comes in trying. Sometimes victory is found in overcoming the trials and tribulations of the quest. Sometimes a person's true character and heart determine or have a direct influence on the end results.

Those who do what they love to do receive payment and recognition of the highest order, self-satisfaction, happiness, and values far exceeding any monetary compensation or praise of others.

Love is the greatest motivator of all time. Do what you love and love what you do to find real, long-lasting satisfaction and true happiness. When you love what you're doing, you will always do your best, finding a way to succeed no matter how long it takes or how difficult a task or goal appears. People who love what they do tend to look for a ray of hope, even in the darkness of the most discouraging of times. Dreams become reality when self-motivated by the strongest force on earth: love.

About the Authors

Surfing experts and identical twins Milton Willis and Michael Willis are internationally recognized for surfing the world's largest waves. Both are expert surfboard shapers and certified professional rescuers. They have taught thousands to successfully surf using their revolutionary "WBsurfing" method and currently operate surfing schools in Hawaii and California.

Published articles by the Willis brothers have appeared in magazines and newspapers worldwide, including *Surfer* (USA), *Trip* (Brazil), and *The Surfer's Path* (UK). The Willises write a weekly syndicated surfing column for the *Del Mar Times* and the *La Jolla Light* newspapers. They also appear or are featured in numerous movies, videos, books, magazines, and television programs.

Milton and Michael are often asked to consult on books, films, and other projects where accurate and insightful surfing information is needed. In addition, they are frequently requested to speak at schools, corporations, and private enterprises about their "land surfing" and "big waves" life-skills programs. Motivational, inspirational, informative, educational, and always entertaining, the Willis brothers show others how to live their dreams and accomplish their goals using the same principles needed to successfully surf large waves. Through their writing, teaching, consulting, and lecturing, they hope the spirit and philosophy of surfing will have a positive effect on family, personal, work, and community relationships.